Chefs and Cooks

by Panky Snow

Consultant:
Walter E. Rhea, CMPC, CEC, CCE, AAC
Executive Director
The American Culinary Federation, Inc.

Bridgestone Books
an imprint of Capstone Press
Mankato, Minnesota

Bridgestone Books are published by Capstone Press
151 Good Counsel Drive, P.O. Box 669, Mankato, Minnesota 56002
http://www.capstone-press.com

Library of Congress Cataloging-in-Publication Data
Snow, Panky.
    Chefs and cooks/by Panky Snow.
    p. cm—(Community helpers)
    Includes bibliographical references and index.
    ISBN 0-7368-0955-4
    1. Cooks—Juvenile literature. 2. Cookery—Juvenile literature. [1. Cooks.
2. Occupations.] I. Title. II. Community helpers (Mankato, MN.)
TX652.5 .S58 2002
641.5′023—dc21
                                                      00-012540

Summary: A simple introduction to the work chefs and cooks do, including where they
    work, tools they use, and their importance to the communities they serve.

Editorial Credits
Sarah Lynn Schuette, editor; Karen Risch, product planning editor; Linda Clavel,
    cover designer; Heidi Schoof, photo researcher

Photo Credits
David F. Clobes, Stock Photography, 18
Jeff Greenberg/Photo Agora, 8
Photo Network, 20
Ron Solomon/Pictor, 16
Rubberball Productions, 10, 12
Shaffer Photography/James L. Shaffer, 6
Unicorn Stock Photos/Jeff Greenberg, cover; Gerold Lim, 14
Visuals Unlimited/Jeff Greenberg, 4

1 2 3 4 5 6 07 06 05 04 03 02

Table of Contents

Chefs and Cooks

Chefs and cooks prepare food for people to eat. Many chefs and cooks are professionals. They get paid to make food. Other chefs and cooks prepare food for fun.

What Chefs and Cooks Do

Chefs and cooks plan menus. They follow recipes or create new recipes. Recipes are directions for making food. Chefs and cooks measure ingredients. They mix ingredients together. Chefs and cooks prepare and serve many types of food.

ingredient
an item of food
used in a recipe

7

Where Chefs and Cooks Work

Chefs and cooks work in large and small kitchens. They often work in schools, restaurants, hospitals, and hotels. They sometimes prepare food for people on trains and ships.

restaurant
a place where people pay for the meals they eat

Types of Chefs and Cooks

Bakers prepare breads, cakes, and pies. Pastry chefs make other desserts. Short-order cooks make fast foods such as hamburgers and french fries. Restaurant chefs make soups, main dishes, and side dishes.

Tools Chefs and Cooks Use

Chefs and cooks use plates, bowls, pots, and pans. They use electric mixers and wooden spoons to stir batter. Chefs and cooks use measuring cups and spoons to measure ingredients. They boil soups on stoves and fry meats on grills.

boil
to heat a liquid until it bubbles

What Chefs and Cooks Wear

Chefs and cooks wear aprons or jackets to keep their clothes clean. They also wear comfortable shoes. Some chefs wear hats to keep their hair out of food.

How Chefs and Cooks Learn

Some people who want to be chefs and cooks go to cooking school. People also learn to cook in their homes. They read cookbooks to find recipes. Many chefs and cooks learn by trying new recipes.

People Who Help Chefs and Cooks

Several people help chefs and cooks.
Dishwashers wash dirty pots, pans,
and dishes. Waiters and waitresses
serve customers the food that chefs
and cooks make. Prep cooks peel and
cut vegetables to use in recipes.

customer
a person who buys goods
or services

How Chefs and Cooks Help Others

Chefs and cooks buy meats, vegetables, and fruits from farmers. School cooks serve healthy food to students. Some chefs and cooks teach others how to prepare certain foods. Chefs and cooks make good food for people to eat.

Hands On: Make Pudding

Chefs and cooks make many different dishes and desserts. You can try to make this dessert.

What You Need

Box of instant chocolate or vanilla pudding
Mixing bowl
Measuring cup
Milk
Egg beater
Peanut butter
Spoon
Chocolate or butterscotch chips
Serving dishes

What You Do

1. Empty the box of pudding into the bowl. Pour 1 3/4 cups cold milk into the bowl and mix with the egg beater.
2. When the pudding begins to get thick, stir 1/2 cup of peanut butter into the bowl. Use the spoon to mix well.
3. Spoon the pudding into serving dishes.
4. Sprinkle the flavored chips on top of the pudding.
5. Serve the pudding to your family.

Words to Know

customer (KUHSS-tuh-mur)—a person who buys goods or services; cooks and chefs make food for customers.

ingredient (in-GREE-dee-uhnt)—an item of food used in a recipe

menu (MEN-yoo)—a list of foods served at a restaurant; chefs and cooks plan menus.

professional (pruh-FESH-uh-nuhl)—someone who is paid to do a job; some chefs and cooks are professionals.

recipe (RESS-i-pee)—directions for making and cooking food

restaurant (RESS-tuh-rahnt)—a place where people pay for the meals they eat; many chefs and cooks work in restaurants.

Read More

Burby, Liza N. *A Day in the Life of a Chef.* The Kids' Career Library. New York: PowerKids Press, 1999.

Quiri, Patricia Ryon. *Chefs.* Community Workers. Minneapolis: Compass Point Books, 2000.

Internet Sites

Cooking with Chef Combo
http://www.nutritionexplorations.org/kids_zone/cooking_with_chef.html

Kids World–Food Safety
http://www.agr.state.nc.us/cyber/kidswrld/foodsafe/index.htm

What Does a Cook Do?
http://www.whatdotheydo.com/cook.htm

Index

aprons, 15
cookbooks, 17
customers, 19
farmers, 21
food, 5, 7, 9, 11, 15, 19, 21
grills, 13
ingredients, 7, 13
kitchens, 9
menus, 7
recipes, 7, 17, 19
stoves, 13
vegetables, 19, 21